D1457103

WARS DAY BY DAY

THE FIRST GULF WAR

1990 – 1991

Steve Crawford

Published by Brown Bear Books Limited

An imprint of
The Brown Reference Group plc
68 Topstone Road
Redding
Connecticut
06896
USA
www.brownreference.com

This hardcover edition is distributed in the United States by:
Black Rabbit Books
P.O. Box 3263
Mankato, MN 56002

ISBN: 978-1-933834-42-9

Library of Congress Cataloging-in-Publication Data

Crawford, Steve, 1960-
The first Gulf War / Steve Crawford.
p. cm.--(Wars day by day)
Summary: "In a time line format, describes the causes leading up to the 1990-1991 Persian Gulf War and political events and battles during the war. Includes primary source quotes"--Provided by publisher.
Includes index.
ISBN 978-1-933834-42-9
1. Persian Gulf War, 1991--Causes. 2. Persian Gulf War, 1991--Campaigns. I. Title.

DS79.72.C73 2009
956.7044'2--dc22

2007050384

Designer: Reg Cox
Creative Director: Jeni Child
Children's Publisher: Anne O'Daly
Editorial Director: Lindsey Lowe
Editor: Peter Darman

Printed and bound in the United States

Photographic credits:
Front Cover: Department of Defense.
Corbis: David Rubinger 17; Michael S. Yamashita 30; Owen Franken 16t; Peter Turnley 15b; Reuters 16b; Sygma/Alain Nogues 10b; Sygma/Jacques Langevin 5; **Department of Defense:** 6, 8t, 9, 10t, 11, 12t, 12b, 13, 15t, 18t, 18b, 19, 20t, 21, 23t, 24, 25t, 26t, 27, 28t, 28b, 29, 31t, 31b, 32t, 33, 34, 35t, 36t, 36b, 37, 38t, 38b, 39, 40t, 40b, 41, 42t, 42b, 43, 44b, 45; **Getty Images:** AFP 8b; Ramzi Haidar 35b; Time & Life Pictures 23b; **PA Photos:** AP 7t; AP/Dominique Mollard 14; AP/Peter Da Jong 22; **Rex Features:** Peter Brooker 25b; TopFoto: Nano Calvo 7b; Picturepoint 44t; UPP 20b.
Back cover: Department of Defense.

Introduction

The Persian Gulf is an arm of the Indian Ocean that divides the Arabian Peninsula from Iran and Central Asia. It is relatively small—but it is one of the most important parts of the world. The reason is oil. Between them, the countries around the Gulf produce 28 percent of the world's oil and are home to over half of its oil reserves. These countries—Bahrain, Iran, Iraq, Kuwait, Qatar, Saudi Arabia, and the United Arab Emirates—grew wealthy in the late 20th century by exporting oil. During the 1980s, Iraq also grew militarily strong. It threatened the entire Persian Gulf region.

Iraq was ruled by Saddam Hussein, who became dictator in 1979. He used the army and police to crush opposition to his rule. He was particularly brutal toward Iraq's minorities: the Kurds in the north, who wanted to create their own country, and the Marsh Arabs in the south. Saddam was also suspicious of Iraqis who followed the Shi'a branch of Islam. Saddam and his colleagues followed the Sunni branch of Islam, but most Iraqis were Shi'ites. Many wanted to be part of neighboring Iran, which was also Shi'ite.

Saddam Hussein greatly enlarged the Iraqi Army, which frightened his neighbors. He also began nuclear, biological, and chemical (NBC) weapons research. Nuclear weapons cause a massive explosion and release radiation. Biological weapons spread diseases, while chemical weapons release poison gas into the air.

The Iran–Iraq War

In 1980 Saddam attacked Iran, where strict Shi'ites had seized power in a revolution. The following Iran–Iraq War (1980–1988) ended without a decisive victory. By its end, however, the Iraqi Army had grown to one million soldiers and had 5,700 tanks. Iraq had spent billions of dollars buying weapons from other countries. A lot of the money for the war had come as loans from Iraq's neighbors, including Kuwait. By 1988, Iraq was $80 billion in debt.

Although Iraq had considerable oil reserves of its own, it could not pay its debts. The problem became worse in 1990, when Kuwait and other Gulf states began to lower prices and increase production. This reduced the price Iraq got for selling its own oil. To make matters worse, Iraq suspected that the Kuwaitis were drilling from their side of the border to tap into Iraqi oil reserves. Saddam Hussein claimed that he had saved the entire region from the spread of Iranian power and that his neighbors were in his debt. He wanted the Kuwaitis to cancel Iraq's debt. Kuwait refused.

After its eight-year war with Iran, Iraq was broke. The Iraqis therefore invaded oil-rich Kuwait to the south.

Kuwaiti oil refineries were some of the main targets taken over by Iraq when it invaded Kuwait in August 1990.

Cash shortages were making it difficult for Saddam to keep up his military strength. He decided that the best response was a rapid takeover of Kuwait. Iraq's neighbor was small. It had only 1.9 million citizens and a tiny army. During late July 1990, Saddam built up his forces on the Kuwaiti border. On August 2, 1990, the elite Iraq Republican Guard invaded. The country was conquered in a few hours.

The United States acts

The Western powers now grew concerned that Saddam also intended to invade Saudi Arabia. That would leave him in control of over half the world's oil reserves. The United States and Kuwaiti officials requested a meeting of the United Nations (UN) Security Council, based in New York. The Council was made up of the United States, Soviet Union, China, France, and Britain. On August 2, 1990, the Security Council passed Resolution 660. This demanded the withdrawal of Iraqi troops from Kuwait. Four days later, it passed Resolution 661, which placed sanctions, or trade restrictions, on Iraq.

On August 7, 1990, U.S. forces moved into Saudi Arabia to protect the country from an Iraqi attack. Eventually, 500,000 U.S. soldiers would be sent to Saudi Arabia. In total, 33 other countries sent 160,000 troops to join the UN forces to free Kuwait from Iraqi rule. But Saddam Hussein would not leave Kuwait. The stage was set for the First Gulf War.

EYEWITNESS: Mikhail Gorbachev, president of the USSR, August 1990

"I think it was the government of England and Margaret Thatcher that from the very beginning preferred military action. That was their style. I do not want to condemn them, but I did not share that approach. We already had the experience of Afghanistan, Vietnam, Namibia, Nicaragua. It only led to bigger conflicts, bigger casualties, bigger destruction, when we neglected our environment, food, and problems in the world."

AUGUST 2 Kuwait

The Iraqi Army invades Kuwait. At 01:00 hours, three divisions of the elite Republican Guard (more than 50,000 soldiers) cross the border. Kuwait has only 16,000 soldiers, and resistance is nearly nonexistent. The Guard reaches the outskirts of the capital, Kuwait City, in just four and a half hours. The attack on the city is supported by airborne special forces troops. The Kuwaitis are crushed and Saddam Hussein proclaims his conquest of Kuwait. Once the Republican Guard has secured all of the strategic points in Kuwait, it moves south to the Kuwait–Saudi Arabia border.

A Saudi F-15 fighter aircraft takes to the skies in August 1990.

Division – a military unit of 15,000 to 20,000 soldiers.

An Iraqi tank on the streets of Kuwait City in August 1990.

AUGUST 2 United States

The United Nations (UN) Security Council holds an emergency session at the request of Kuwait and the United States. It votes 14–0 (with Yemen abstaining) to condemn the invasion of Kuwait and to demand that Iraq withdraw immediately.

AUGUST 2 Indian Ocean

The U.S. aircraft carrier USS *Independence* sails toward the Persian Gulf to aid the Saudis.

AUGUST 2 United States

The UN Security Council places a trade embargo on Iraq. This prevents Iraq from selling its goods to or buying goods from other countries.

AUGUST 2 Saudi Arabia

The Saudi ruler, King Fahd, has only 70,000 troops. He requests aid from his ally, the United States. The Americans are determined to prevent Saddam Hussein taking over Saudi Arabia. The Iraqis already control more than 20 percent of the world's oil reserves. If the Iraqis conquer Saudi Arabia, they will control more than half the world's oil supplies. U.S. aircraft and warships set out to help support the Saudis.

AUGUST 6 Kuwait

There are now 11 Iraqi Army divisions in Kuwait. They can overrun Saudi Arabia with ease if Saddam Hussein orders an invasion. But the order is not given.

TURNING POINTS: The United Nations

The Gulf War is an example of the role the United Nations (UN; headquarters at right) plays in trying to prevent international conflict. When Iraq invaded Kuwait, the UN voted to limit Iraq's economy by barring its international trade. The UN's Security Council then voted to use force to remove Iraq from Kuwait. The United States, because of the size of its armed forces, assumed the lead role in providing troops and aid to fight Iraqi aggression, but it remained part of a UN-organized coalition of nations.

Coalition – an alliance of nations.

The guided-missile cruiser USS *Ticonderoga* on the way to the Gulf.

AUGUST 7 Saudi Arabia
Saudi Arabia formally requests U.S. troops to help defend itself against a possible Iraqi attack. The first U.S. forces arrive in the country. They are F-15 Eagle fighter aircraft from Langley Air Force Base, Virginia. The jets are the spearhead of Operation Desert Shield, the codename for the U.S. defense of Saudi Arabia.

AUGUST 8 Iraq
Saddam Hussein proclaims the takeover of Kuwait.

AUGUST 9 United States
The UN outlaws the Iraqi conquest of Kuwait.

AUGUST 10 Iraq
Saddam Hussein declares a "jihad," or Muslim holy war, against the United States and Israel. He aims to win the support of Muslims in the region. Many are hostile to Israel and its ally, the United States. However, most Muslims do not support Saddam Hussein.

AUGUST 12 Persian Gulf
A UN naval blockade of Iraq begins. All shipments of Iraqi oil to international customers

IN FOCUS: Hostages

In August 1990, Iraq announced that it would "play host" to the 11,000 foreigners in the country. In effect, the foreigners could not leave. Saddam Hussein (at right, with a British hostage) spread hostages around the country to prevent any UN attempt to rescue them. Some were imprisoned in military bases as so-called "human shields." The Iraqis hoped that the UN would not bomb bases where hostages might be killed. After widespread international criticism, Iraq released the hostages in December.

Blockade – to stop enemy ships leaving their ports.

EYEWITNESS: Margaret Thatcher, British prime minister, August 1990

"Oil is vital to the economy of the world. If you didn't stop him, and didn't turn him back, he would have gone over the border to Saudi Arabia, and right down the west side of the Gulf and in fact could have got control of 65 percent of the world's oil reserves, from which he could have blackmailed every nation. So there were two things, aggressors must be stopped, and he must not get control of this oil."

are halted by Coalition warships patrolling the waters of the Persian Gulf.

AUGUST 12 Saudi Arabia
A U.S. Air Force sergeant becomes the first death of Operation Desert Shield when he is hit by a military truck in a traffic accident.

AUGUST 22 United States
U.S. President George H.W. Bush begins the first call-up of selected reservists (part-time soldiers) for active duty in the Persian Gulf. They will serve for 90 days. This is the first such call-up in the United States since the Vietnam War in the 1960s.

AUGUST 25 United States
The UN Security Council approves the use of force against ships trying to dodge the blockade of Iraq. UN warships in the Gulf can now sink Iraqi ships if necessary.

AUGUST 28 Iraq
Iraq declares Kuwait its 19th province and renames Kuwait City al-Kadhima.

AUGUST 28 Syria
Mass pro-Iraqi demonstrations take place throughout the country.

AUGUST 31 Iraq
Western male civilians working in Iraq have not been allowed to leave the country. They are moved to Iraq's most important military sites to act as "human shields." The Iraqis believe that Allied aircraft will not attack these sites because the Allies will be frightened of killing the Western hostages.

U.S. soldiers wait to board a plane that will take them to Saudi Arabia.

Reservist – part-time soldier.

Troops of the French Foreign Legion in Saudi Arabia in the fall of 1990.

SEPTEMBER 12 United States
U.S. President George Bush speaks to Congress. He stresses the international cooperation taking place with regard to the Gulf crisis.

SEPTEMBER 14–15 Kuwait
Iraqi troops raid the homes of the ambassadors from France, Canada, Tunisia, and Bangladesh. They also enter the compound of the Belgian Embassy. Such actions are illegal under international law.

SEPTEMBER 14–15 Europe
Britain and France announce that they are sending 12,000 soldiers, 168 tanks, and bombers and helicopters to join Coalition forces in the Gulf. Also, Japan and Germany pledge more money to the Coalition.

OCTOBER 1 Saudi Arabia
Defense Minister Prince Sultan bin Abdul Aziz declares that if Iraqi troops withdraw from Kuwait, all foreign forces will leave Saudi Arabia.

OCTOBER 7 Israel
Israeli authorities start giving out gas masks to civilians. The crisis in the Gulf, and the threats made against Israel by Iraq, make the Israelis frightened of a chemical weapons attack.

KEY PEOPLE: Saddam Hussein

Saddam Hussein was ruler of Iraq from 1979 until 2003, when he was overthrown by the United States. He had joined the Baath Party while he was a student. In 1958, he murdered a supporter of Iraq's then ruler. By 1979 Saddam was dictator of Iraq. He then started a war with Iran that lasted eight years. In August 1990 he ordered the invasion of Kuwait. Although defeated by the UN in February 1991, he remained in power in Iraq.

Dictator – a ruler who has no restraints on his or her power.

EYEWITNESS: Tariq Aziz, Iraqi foreign minister, August 1990

"We were pushed into a fatal struggle in the sense of a struggle in which your fate will be decided. You will either be hit inside your house and destroyed, economically and militarily. Or you go outside and attack the enemy in one of his bases. We had to do that, we had no choice. Iraq was designated by President George Bush for destruction, with or without Kuwait. Inside Kuwait or outside Kuwait."

OCTOBER 26 Saudi Arabia
U.S. troop levels in Saudi Arabia now stand at 300,000. President Bush's advisors stop referring to the operation in Saudi Arabia as "Desert Shield." They now call it "Desert Sword," as a sign that they are building up forces to free Kuwait.

OCTOBER 29 United States
The UN Security Council passes Resolution 674. This states that force can be used against Iraq if it continues to occupy Kuwait. It also holds Iraq responsible for all damages and injuries caused by its invasion, and calls for Iraq to pay compensation for damages and injuries.

Armored vehicles of the British Army near the Kuwait border in October.

Compound – a walled-in area.

NOVEMBER 3 Iraq
A senior politician in the Iraqi National Assembly says that Iraq will free all Western hostages if the United States and other Coalition members promise not to attack Iraqi troops.

One of the large tent camps built by the U.S. Army in Saudi Arabia.

NOVEMBER 8 United States
President George Bush orders 100,000 extra U.S. troops to the Persian Gulf. He says that the 300,000 troops already there are enough to defend Saudi Arabia but not enough to free Kuwait.

NOVEMBER 12 United States
U.S. reservists (part-time soldiers) have their period of duty doubled, to 180 days.

NOVEMBER 16 Iraq
Saddam Hussein says that the Gulf crisis will only be solved by talks between Iraq and the United States or Saudi Arabia. However, he still refuses to order a withdrawal from Kuwait.

NOVEMBER 18 Iraq
President Saddam Hussein says that Iraq will begin freeing Western hostages over a three-month period, beginning on December 25,

TURNING POINTS: Desert Warfare

Most of the Gulf War was fought in sandy or stony deserts. Fighting in such conditions is very difficult. The high daytime temperatures mean that soldiers must drink lots of water to stay alert. But at night it gets very cold, and so troops also need plenty of blankets and warm clothing. The desert terrain is also a problem for vehicles and aircraft. Dust and small stones, thrown up by exhausts and helicopter rotor blades (at right), can get into engines, which causes mechanical breakdowns.

Nonaggression – a refusal to use force.

EYEWITNESS: Lieutenant M. T. Mulvenin, Saudi Arabia, 1990

"We are getting more heaters. You know, we couldn't have envisioned that it was going to be cold over here (in Saudi Arabia) like it's been. But when we got over here from the United States, it was 120, 125 degrees. And now we've had some mornings, especially up north, near the Kuwait border, where it's below freezing. So everybody brought their sleeping bags and a field jacket. That's the desert. Hot by day and freezing by night."

unless anything "mars the atmosphere of peace." U.S. Secretary of State James Baker rejects the offer. British Foreign Secretary Douglas Hurd says the hostages should be freed immediately.

NOVEMBER 29 United States
The UN Security Council authorizes use of "all means necessary" to throw Iraqi forces out of Kuwait. This would allow the Coalition to use military force against the Iraqis.

NOVEMBER 30 United States
President George Bush offers to send Secretary of State James Baker to Iraq for talks. Afterward, Iraqi Foreign Minister Tariq Aziz will be invited to visit the United States. Iraq rejects the offer.

DECEMBER 3 Saudi Arabia
Some 20 U.S. F-117 Stealth Fighter aircraft land in Saudi Arabia as part of Operation Desert Sword.

DECEMBER 6 Iraq
Saddam Hussein says that all Western hostages in Iraq and Kuwait can go home. Other countries have been very critical of Iraq's hostage-taking, so Saddam is eager to keep the little international support he still has.

DECEMBER 17 United States
The UN declares that all Iraqi forces must leave Kuwait by January 15, 1991, but Saddam Hussein rejects all UN resolutions concerned with Kuwait. Unless Saddam backs down, war between Iraq and the UN Coalition is likely to break out in the new year.

Giant U.S Abrams tanks are unloaded from a ship in a Saudi port.

Hostage – a person held captive against his or her will.

JANUARY 9 Switzerland
Talks take place in Geneva, the Swiss capital, between U.S. Secretary of State James Baker and Iraqi Foreign Minister Tariq Aziz. The talks aim to end the Gulf crisis peacefully, but they end in stalemate.

JANUARY 12 United States
The United States Congress grants President George Bush authority to go to war to end Iraq's occupation of Kuwait.

JANUARY 15 Kuwait
The date given by the UN Security Council for Iraq to leave Kuwait comes and goes without any movement by Iraqi forces.

JANUARY 16 Iraq
Operation Desert Storm begins. Coalition warplanes attack Iraqi targets in Kuwait and Iraq. The first attacks destroy most of Iraq's antiaircraft defenses. Helicopters attack Iraqi radar installations. Iraqi command-and-control centers in the capital, Baghdad, are attacked by F-117 Stealth Fighters and Tomahawk cruise missiles. Iraqi air bases and aircraft hangars are also bombed. In Kuwait, Coalition aircraft attack hundreds of reinforced shelters where Iraqi troops are hiding.

EYEWITNESS: Wafic al Samarrai, Iraqi intelligence

"Iraq left the war with Iran heavily in debt. Toward the end of the Iraq-Iran War the Iraqi Army stood at 1.2 million soldiers and had more than 5,800 tanks and more than 600 combat aircraft and many pieces of artillery. In addition, this includes the popular army. Saddam Hussein thought that Kuwait was the salvation from the poor economic state that resulted from the war with Iran."

Baghdad, the capital of Iraq, is hit by Coalition bombs on January 16.

JANUARY 16 United States
President Bush declares, "We will not fail." He orders the Federal Bureau of Investigation (FBI) to track down some 3,000 Iraqis whose visas have expired. The government is worried that some of the Iraqis may launch terrorist attacks against the United States.

JANUARY 17 Iraq
The Coalition again bombs Baghdad. Saddam Hussein tells the Iraqi people: "The great showdown has begun! The mother of all battles is underway."

Terrorist – an extremist who uses violence against civilians.

A U.S. warship fires a Tomahawk cruise missile.

JANUARY 17 Saudi Arabia
Iraqi artillery shells an oil refinery near the Kuwait border. U.S. aircraft retaliate.

JANUARY 18 United States
President Bush tells the nation that the air war will destroy Iraq's ability to make nuclear weapons. It also aims to destroy Iraq's chemical weapons and to free Kuwait. Bush authorizes the call-up of one million National Guardsmen and reservists to serve for up to two years.

JANUARY 18 Iraq
Iraq fires two Scud missiles. One hits Israel while another, fired at Saudi Arabia, is shot down by a U.S. Patriot air-defense missile. President Bush says Israel has promised not to respond to Iraq's attack. The Allies report losing three aircraft in the first 24 hours of Operation Desert Storm. Refugees begin heading for Jordan to escape the conflict.

JANUARY 18 Japan
The Iraqi ambassador to Japan warns that Iraq reserves the right to use chemical weapons in the war.

IN FOCUS: Refugees

There were tens of thousands of non-Iraqi workers in Iraq in 1990. When war with the Coalition seemed likely, thousands fled to neighboring Jordan. These included Jordanians, Palestinians, and more than 30,000 Iraqi refugees who eventually settled in Jordan. As the Coalition bombing continued, further frightened refugees arrived at the border with Jordan with few belongings (at right). By the end of 1990, there were one million refugees from Iraq living in camps in Jordan.

Refugee – a civilian who flees a war zone.

JANUARY 19 Israel
At least three Iraqi Scud missiles explode in Tel Aviv, injuring 17 people. The United States sends more Patriot missiles to Israel, which announces it is in a state of war. The Coalition fears that Israel will attack Iraq. Such an attack will mean that Arab members of the Coalition will leave the alliance.

One of the many antiwar rallies held in Europe during January 1991.

JANUARY 19 Persian Gulf
U.S. troops liberate nine oil platforms off Kuwait, capturing their first Iraqi prisoners of war.

JANUARY 20 Saudi Arabia
Iraq fires 10 Scuds at Saudi Arabia. Nine are shot down and one falls harmlessly into the sea.

JANUARY 20 Iraq
Seven captured Allied airmen are shown on Iraqi TV. They appear to have been beaten by their captors. Article 17 of the 1949 Geneva Convention states that "no physical or mental torture, nor any other form of coercion, may be inflicted on a prisoner of war." The British Ministry of Defence confirms that a third Royal Air Force (RAF) Tornado bomber has been shot down. UN aircraft losses now stand at 15.

KEY UNITS: The Iraqi Army

The Iraqi Army facing the forces of the UN Coalition was very strong. Saddam Hussein had 1.2 million soldiers, 5,800 tanks, 5,100 other armored vehicles, and 3,850 artillery pieces. However, many Iraqi troops were conscripts who had little enthusiasm for the war. In addition, they had poor equipment and unreliable food supplies. When the air war started in January 1991, Iraqi troops (at right) were bombed everyday. This badly affected their morale. As a result, many did not fight but surrendered.

Conscript – a civilian drafted into the army.

Destroyed buildings in Tel Aviv, Israel, after an Iraqi Scud missile attack.

JANUARY 21 Kuwait
Iraq begins blowing up Kuwaiti oil wells. They will eventually set fire to more than 600 oil wells.

JANUARY 21 Iraq
Iraq fires six Scud missiles at Saudi Arabia. One is destroyed by a Patriot missile and the others fall harmlessly in the desert
.

JANUARY 21 Israel
An Iraqi Scud missile hits Tel Aviv, killing three Israelis.

JANUARY 21 Jordan
Hundreds of Iraqi refugees cross into Jordan. The UN says that up to 750,000 foreigners may be waiting to leave Iraq once it is safe to travel.

JANUARY 20 Israel
Israel confirms it will not retaliate against Iraq.

JANUARY 20 Europe
Antiwar demonstrators storm an army barracks in Berlin, Germany. Demonstrations held in Brussels, Belgium, call for an end to military support for the Coalition.

JANUARY 21 Saudi Arabia
U.S. officials say 8,000 air sorties (missions) have been launched against Iraqi targets.

JANUARY 21 Britain
Defence Secretary Tom King says he suspects that Iraq has used torture to force Allied airmen to make statements. Parliament votes to support British participation in Operation Desert Storm by 563 votes to 34.

JANUARY 21 United States
President Bush declares that Saddam Hussein will be held accountable for the treatment of Coalition prisoners in Iraqi hands.

EYEWITNESS: Rhonda Cornum, captured U.S. medic

"The Iraqis realized I was a woman when they stood me up. At that point I had my flak jacket on and my survival vest and my weapon, all that stuff. So they took off my flight helmet, and all this long shoulder-length brown hair came out. And until then I'm sure they just thought I was a skinny guy. But all of a sudden they realized, 'Oh my, this is a girl!'"

Flak jacket – a jacket that includes bullet-proof armor.

JANUARY 23 Iraq
The British announce that another Tornado bomber has been shot down over Iraq.

JANUARY 24 Saudi Arabia
To show that they still have some operable warplanes, the Iraqis launch an air attack on the major Saudi oil refinery in Abqaiq. Two MiG-23 fighters and two Mirage F-1 fighters carrying incendiary bombs take off from bases in Iraq. However, they are spotted by U.S. Airborne Warning And Control (AWAC) aircraft. Two Saudi Air Force F-15 fighters intercept the Iraqis. The MiGs turn back to Iraq. The Mirages fly on but are shot down by an F-15 flown by Captain Iyad Al-Shamrani.

JANUARY 24 Britain
The British announce the loss of a fifth Tornado. Some 12 RAF Buccaneers and two more army regiments are being sent to the Gulf. The Buccaneers will be used to pinpoint targets on the ground using laser beams. Bombs released by Tornados will then strike the targets "painted" by the lasers.

An American Airborne Warning And Control (AWAC) aircraft in the Gulf.

JANUARY 24 Persian Gulf
British Royal Navy and U.S. Navy ships clash with Iraqi Navy vessels and liberate the Kuwaiti island of Qaruh. The island lies 23 miles (37 km) off the Kuwaiti coast. Three Iraqis are killed and 51 captured in the operation. Two Iraqi warships are also sunk.

JANUARY 25 Persian Gulf
Iraq begins an environmental war by dumping millions of gallons of oil into the Persian Gulf.

KEY PEOPLE: George Bush

Republican George H. W. Bush became the 41st president of the United States in 1989. He had previously served in Congress and been ambassador to the UN, head of the CIA, and vice president. In August 1990, Bush and his advisers organized the international coalition to oppose Iraq's invasion of Kuwait. After the Gulf War, Bush was very popular at home. In 1992, however, he lost the presidential election to Bill Clinton.

CIA – Central Intelligence Agency, a U.S. spy organization.

EYEWITNESS: Terry Walker, British Army, Saudia Arabia, January 1991

"I stuck my head out of the vehicle cab to get some fresh air, and all of a sudden, and without warning, the silence was broken with two huge explosions. The alarms all around the area started to whistle, to scream, and then the air-raid sirens started. There was near panic all around as everyone suddenly realized that we were now the target for Scud missiles. Saddam had certainly scored a point against our technology."

JANUARY 25 Israel
Iraq fires seven Scud missiles at Israel. One person is killed and dozens are injured.

JANUARY 25 Iraq
Allied aircraft losses now total 25 from about 17,500 sorties (missions) flown.

JANUARY 26 Persian Gulf
The oil spill is now 31 miles (50 km) long and 8 miles (12.8 km) wide. The oil threatens Saudi Arabia's desalination plants, which turn saltwater into drinking water. It is also damaging the fragile ecosystem of the Persian Gulf. Meanwhile, the Pentagon, the headquarters of the U.S. Department of Defense, confirms that the submarine USS *Louisville* has launched a cruise missile.

JANUARY 26 Iran
Iraqi warplanes land in Iran to prevent them being destroyed by Allied aircraft. Iran says it has seized the aircraft.

JANUARY 26 Iraq
U.S. F-15 Eagles win the war's first major dogfight. They shoot down three Iraqi MiG-23 fighter aircraft.

JANUARY 26 United States
There are antiwar protests in Washington, D.C., Los Angeles, and San Francisco.

JANUARY 26 Europe
Antiwar demonstrators march in Bonn, Germany, and London, United Kingdom.

JANUARY 26 Kuwait
U.S. Marine 155-mm howitzers fire at Iraqi troops 6 miles (9.6 km) inside Kuwait.

Oil spilled from Kuwaiti wells laps the Saudi coast.

Dogfight – combat between fighter aircraft.

JANUARY 27 Persian Gulf
Coalition warplanes bomb Iraqi-held oil facilities at the Sea Island Terminal in Kuwait to stop Iraq dumping more oil into the Persian Gulf. The oil flow slows to a trickle.

JANUARY 27 United States
Despite fears of terrorism, Super Bowl XXV goes off without a hitch. The game is held at the Tampa Stadium in Tampa, Florida, between the New York Giants and the Buffalo Bills.

JANUARY 27 Jordan
Jordanian officials say that thousands of Iraqi refugees have been ordered to return to Baghdad because they have no exit visas.

An Iraqi radar station in Kuwait destroyed by a Coalition air attack.

JANUARY 27 Iran
The Iranian news reports that oil-polluted rain has fallen on Iran.

JANUARY 27 Iraq
A letter to UN Secretary General Javier Perez de Cuellar from the Iraqi foreign minister is broadcast by Baghdad Radio. It says Iraq will hold the UN official personally responsible for the continuing attacks on its territory. Meanwhile, two U.S. Air Force F-15 warplanes shoot down four Iraqi MiG-23s near Baghdad. The Iraqis have now lost 26 warplanes in dogfights in the war.

KEY PEOPLE: Margaret Thatcher

Margaret Thatcher was the first female British prime minister. When Saddam Hussein invaded Iraq, she urged President Bush to take action. She condemned Saddam as a brutal dictator. If Saddam took Saudi Arabia, she believed, he would have over half the world's oil reserves. She said that Britain and America had to prevent this. Bush agreed. It was largely at Thatcher's urging that the world stood up to the Iraqi aggression.

Landmine – a container filled with explosives that is buried in the ground.

EYEWITNESS: Huda M. al Yassiri, Iraqi journalist, January 1991

"During the early days of the war, Baghdad was more like a dead city, without electricity, telecommunications, or traffic. The city had been hurriedly deserted. Most of its people fled their homes looking for a shelter in the outskirts and nearby villages. Life seemed to have come to a standstill as streets were deserted and shops were closed down. Hospitals were empty except for a few patients, mainly dying children."

JANUARY 27 Kuwait
A U.S. military spokesman says that Iraqi troops have planted an estimated 500,000 landmines inside Kuwait.

JANUARY 28 Iran
More than 80 Iraqi aircraft, including at least 39 warplanes, are reported to have flown to Iran. The Iraqis are hoping to prevent them being destroyed by Coalition aircraft. They hope to get them back when the war is over.

JANUARY 28 Britain
Britain urgently flies antipollution equipment to Saudi Arabia to defend the coastline and desalination plants from oil slicks.

JANUARY 28 Jordan
The UN Disaster Relief Organization says 9,800 refugees have now been allowed to cross the border into Jordan from Iraq.

JANUARY 28 United States
President George Bush says that the United States does not seek the destruction or destabilization of Iraq. He states that U.S. forces will leave the Gulf when their mission to free Kuwait ends.

JANUARY 28 Saudi Arabia
Some 24,000 sorties have now been flown by Coalition aircraft. The U.S. Department of Defense announces: "Iraq is unable to offer any organized air resistance."

JANUARY 28 Kuwait
Coalition warplanes destroy 24 Iraqi tanks, armored personnel carriers, and trucks.

An Iraqi bunker inside Kuwait explodes after being hit by bombs.

Sortie – a mission flown by a warplane.

U.S. troops rest near their armored vehicle during the Battle of Khafji.

JANUARY 29 Kuwait

Iraqi mechanized forces cross the border and fight U.S. and other Coalition troops near the town of Al Wafra. U.S. Cobra helicopter gunships and warplanes help to defeat the Iraqis, who lose 10 tanks. Coalition forces lose three armored vehicles in the battle.

JANUARY 29 Saudi Arabia

Near the town of Khafji, Iraqi armored fighting vehicles attack Coalition forces after having given the impression that they were about to surrender. U.S. helicopter gunships fire missiles and destroy four Iraqi tanks and 13 other vehicles in the ongoing battle.

EYEWITNESS: Commander D. G. Morral, captain of the U.S.S. *Nicholas*

"The mission at the beginning of hostilities for the *Nicholas* was to get as far north as possible so that we could stand by to relieve the pilots who were shot down. That's why we're so far forward from the rest of the ships. From that forward position, then, if pilots went down we could pick them out of the water, which we did in January. In late January we picked an F-16 pilot out of the water off Kuwait Bay."

Mechanized – describing military forces that are transported in vehicles.

JANUARY 29 Persian Gulf
British, U.S., and Saudi naval vessels attack 17 Iraqi patrol boats off the island of Maradin. Five of the Iraqi boats are sunk and the remainder head for the Kuwaiti coastline.

An Iraqi tank that was destroyed during the Battle of Khafji in January.

JANUARY 30 Saudi Arabia
The Battle of Khafji is over. The 15th Iraqi Mechanized Infantry Brigade had attacked the small town of Khafji. The battle with Coalition forces that followed resulted in the deaths of 11 U.S. Marines. But 24 Iraqi tanks were destroyed in all, along with 13 other armored vehicles.

JANUARY 31 Saudi Arabia
Saudi and Qatari troops, backed by U.S. artillery, recapture Khafji from the Iraqis. Some 2,600 sorties are flown by Coalition aircraft today.

JANUARY 31 Persian Gulf
Some 17 Iraqi patrol boats are sunk when they are attacked by British RAF Jaguar ground-attack aircraft and British Royal Navy Lynx helicopters armed with missiles. By the end of January, nearly 80 Iraqi naval vessels have been sunk in the war.

KEY WEAPONS: Scud missile

During the war, the Iraqis fired Scud missiles at Israel. The Scud was first used by the Soviet Union in the 1960s. It consisted of a warhead on top of a fuel container. The warhead could be either explosive or nuclear, although Iraq did not have any nuclear weapons. The Scud had a range of up to 500 miles (800 km). The missile could be fired from the back of a truck or a static launch site (at right). The Scud had only a basic guidance system and was not very accurate.

Guidance system – computers and sensors that steer a missile.

EYEWITNESS: John R. Vines, U.S. 82nd Airborne Division

"And one of the things that strikes you is how the Iraqis deploy their defenses. You'll have minefields and then you'll have wire. And then you'll have tank ditches or get to a tank ditch first. And the depth between them were really killing zones. It takes a lot out of you if you're having to move through heavy sand and perhaps carrying heavy rucksacks."

FEBRUARY 1 United States
Secretary of Defense Dick Cheney warns that the United States will retaliate if Iraq uses chemical or biological weapons in the Gulf. The State Department reveals that 70 terrorist attacks have been carried out against countries supporting the UN Coalition since the war began. Some have been by pro-Iraqi groups.

FEBRUARY 1 Saudi Arabia
An Iraqi FROG long-range missile fired at the positions of the U.S. 82nd Airborne Division lands harmlessly in the mud.

FEBRUARY 1 Iraq
Coalition aircraft attack the towns of Basra, Faw, Abdul Khasid, and Az-Zubair. Iraqi radio accuses UN pilots of bombing civilian targets and machine-gunning people in the streets.

This road bridge in Kuwait was destroyed by an air strike.

FROG missile – a short-range battlefield missile.

U.S. Harrier strike aircraft on patrol in the skies over Iraq in February.

FEBRUARY 1 France
France gives its permission for U.S. B-52 Stratofortress bombers to overfly its land during missions against Iraq. It also grants permission for tanker aircraft to use French bases to refuel the B-52s in flight. So far, five B-52 missions have been flown in the war.

FEBRUARY 2 Israel
Two Iraqi Scuds hit central Israel. There are no casualties.

FEBRUARY 3 Kuwait
The Americans announce that 25 of the 30 major bridges out of Kuwait have been destroyed by Coalition air strikes. This has interrupted the flow of supplies, such as food and fuel, to Iraqi units based in Kuwait.

FEBRUARY 3 Iran
A high-ranking Islamic leader in Iran, Ayatollah Mohammed-Reza Golpayegani, writes to President George Bush urging the withdrawal of U.S. troops from the Gulf. Golpayegani says that attacks on the Iraqi people will have serious consequences. He also condemns Iraq's occupation of Kuwait.

FEBRUARY 3 Morocco
Thousands of Moroccans stage a pro-Iraq demonstration in the capital, Rabat.

TURNING POINTS: The impact of television

The Gulf War was one of the first conflicts in which the world watched a military conflict unfold via global TV satellite networks. Television viewers were fascinated when missiles lit up the night sky over Baghdad. The British and Americans used television to reveal Iraqi crimes, such as the release of oil into the Gulf. This increased the public's support for the war. The Iraqis used TV to show off captured Coalition troops (at right). This bolstered support within Iraq, but upset many viewers outside.

Killing zone – an area of the battlefield always covered by enemy fire.

FEBRUARY 3 Persian Gulf
The battleship USS *Missouri* fires at Iraqi positions inside Kuwait in support of U.S. Marine and other Coalition ground troops. This is the first time the ship has fired in combat since the Korean War (1950–1953).

General Colin Powell (left) and General Norman Schwarzkopf (right).

FEBRUARY 4 Kuwait
U.S. Marine Corps aircraft destroy 25 Iraqi tanks with missiles and bombs.

FEBRUARY 5 Iraq
Iraq halts gasoline sales to civilians. This creates heating and transport problems.

FEBRUARY 5 Saudi Arabia
Syrian troops push back Iraqi forces on the Saudi-Kuwait border. Czechoslovakia sends 37 more soldiers to Saudi Arabia.

FEBRUARY 5 Britain
U.S. B-52 bombers begin arriving at the RAF base at Fairford.

FEBRUARY 5 USSR
The Soviet foreign minister calls upon Iraq to restore Kuwait's independence. He says that the war is getting out of control and that Baghdad is being damaged beyond repair.

FEBRUARY 5 France
The French defense minister confirms that French troops will participate in any coming UN ground offensive, including any invasion of Iraqi territory.

KEY UNITS: Special forces

Before Coalition forces launched the ground war in February 1991, American and British special forces went into Iraq and Kuwait. They were from the British Special Air Service (SAS) and U.S. Delta Force. Their task was to discover where enemy soldiers and vehicles were hidden. They also tried to find Iraqi Scud missiles. The special forces soldiers traveled in vehicles such as the Fast Attack Vehicle (at right) and Land Rover. The vehicles were armed with machine guns and rocket launchers.

Special forces – soldiers trained to fight behind enemy lines.

The battleship USS *Wisconsin* fires on Iraqi positions from the Persian Gulf.

FEBRUARY 6 Iraq
U.S. F-15 fighters shoot down four Iraqi warplanes as they try to join 120 Iraqi aircraft fleeing to Iran. U.S. F-16 ground-attack aircraft have now switched from using bombs to firing Maverick antitank missiles against Iraqi Republican Guard and tank formations in Kuwait and Iraq.

FEBRUARY 6 United States
President Bush assures Pakistan's president, who is a Muslim, that Coalition forces will show respect for Iraq's holy places by not bombing them.

FEBRUARY 6 Persian Gulf
The battleship USS *Wisconsin*, taking over from its sistership USS *Missouri*, fires 11 shells and destroys an Iraqi artillery battery located in southern Kuwait.

FEBRUARY 7 United States
President Bush's top two war advisers, Defense Secretary Dick Cheney and Joint Chiefs Chairman Colin Powell, leave for the Gulf region to assess the UN war effort.

FEBRUARY 7 Saudi Arabia
The British commander-in-chief in the Gulf, General Sir Peter de la Billière, says that he believes a ground offensive against the Iraqi Army to free Kuwait is now inevitable.

FEBRUARY 7 Persian Gulf
USS *Wisconsin* continues to shell Iraqi artillery and naval sites in Kuwait with its giant 16 in (406 mm) guns. It sinks 15 Iraqi boats at Khawr al-Mufattah Marina.

EYEWITNESS: Saddam Hussein, president of Iraq, February 1991

"What remains for Bush and his accomplices in crime is to understand that they are personally responsible for their crime. The Iraqi people will pursue them for this crime, even if they leave office. There is no doubt they will understand what we mean if they know what revenge means to the Arabs. Every Iraqi child, woman, and old man knows how to take revenge. They will avenge the pure blood that has been shed."

Battleship – a large, heavily armed warship.

KEY WEAPONS: Stealth aircraft

The U.S. Air Force had 36 F-117 Nighthawk Stealth Fighters (at right). Although a tiny percentage of the force of 1,900 Coalition fighters and bombers, the fighters played a key role. They are coated with a secret, radar-absorbent material, so cannot be detected by radar. F-117s attacked Baghdad on many occasions. The city was protected by more than 3,000 antiaircraft guns and 60 missile batteries, but no Stealth Fighter was shot down over the city. In fact, no F-117 was lost during the war.

FEBRUARY 8 Iraq
The Iraqi Army begins to suffer desertions as a result of the Coalition bombing campaign.

FEBRUARY 8 Saudi Arabia
The commander of U.S. and UN forces in the Gulf, General Norman Schwarzkopf, says it is too early to tell if a ground war will be needed to free Kuwait.

FEBRUARY 8 Holland
The Netherlands announces that it is to supply Israel with eight Patriot missile launchers as a defense against ongoing Iraqi Scud attacks.

FEBRUARY 8 Persian Gulf
A British Royal Navy helicopter destroys an Iraqi patrol boat near Faylakah Island.

FEBRUARY 8 Iran
A further 13 Iraqi aircraft land in Iran. This brings the total number of Iraqi aircraft in Iran to 147. Of these, 121 are fighter aircraft. Iran will not return any of these aircraft to Iraq when the war is over.

FEBRUARY 9 Saudi Arabia
U.S. Defense Secretary Dick Cheney and Joint Chiefs Chairman Colin Powell meet for more than eight hours with the Coalition commander, General Schwarzkopf and other military leaders. They talk about plans for a ground offensive against the Iraqis.

A Patriot missile launch site. Patriots were used to shoot down Scuds.

Joint Chiefs – a group of officers from each branch of the U.S. armed forces.

EYEWITNESS: General Sir Peter de la Billière, British Army

"We were faced with the fourth largest army in the world, the fifth largest air force in the world. They'd been fighting for eight years, and must have had an enormous amount of battle experience, and they were used to operating in that terrain, which of course, to our western European forces, was alien. I don't think we ever thought we weren't going to win. We were going to win at a price. But how big was that price going to be?"

FEBRUARY 9 Israel

An Iraqi Scud missile attack against Tel Aviv injures 25 people.

FEBRUARY 9 Syria

An official Syrian newspaper urges Iraqis to kill Saddam Hussein to end the war.

FEBRUARY 10 Iraq

Saddam Hussein addresses the nation. He promises victory and praises "steadfastness, faith, and light in the chests of Iraqis." But today, 2,900 Coalition sorties are flown against Iraqi targets.

FEBRUARY 10 Saudi Arabia

The Saudis reopen a desalination plant at Safania which had been closed due to the drifting oil slick. U.S. Defense Secretary Cheney states that the war is going well and that Iraqi production facilities for nuclear, biological, and chemical (NBC) weapons have been almost destroyed. But he admits that Iraq still has chemical weapons and says there will be no halt in attacks until Kuwait is free.

FEBRUARY 11 Turkey

The Turks assure Syria, Egypt, and Saudi Arabia that they have no plans to seize Iraqi territory. Turkey shares a border with northern Iraq. Some Gulf states are worried that Turkey will take advantage of an Iraqi defeat to conquer parts of northern Iraq.

FEBRUARY 11 Israel

Iraq fires two Scud missiles at Israel. One is shot down by a Patriot missile. The other hits a residential area, injuring 30 people.

A U.S. Air Force technician checks bombs before they are fixed to aircraft.

B-52 – U.S. eight-engined heavy bomber.

Coalition bombs hit this bunker in Baghdad, killing 400 people.

FEBRUARY 12 Jordan
Officials say Syria and Yemen are to supply oil to Jordan. The imports will solve shortages caused by the Gulf crisis, which has halted all oil shipments from Iraq.

FEBRUARY 12 Persian Gulf
The battleship USS *Missouri* shells Iraqi troops, artillery, a command bunker, and tanks in southern Kuwait. The vessel fires 60 shells in the bombardment.

FEBRUARY 13 Iraq
A Coalition bombing raid against Baghdad destroys three major bridges and kills 400 people in an air-raid shelter. The shelter is hit by two laser-guided bombs. Coalition commanders say that they thought the shelter was a camouflaged command-and-control bunker. The incident leads to restrictions on the Coalition strategic bombing campaign.

FEBRUARY 14 United States
The Pentagon says that Coalition warplanes have destroyed at least 1,300 of Iraq's 4,280 tanks, 800 of its 2,870 armored vehicles, and 1,100 of its 3,110 artillery pieces.

FEBRUARY 14 Saudi Arabia
Two Iraqi Scud missiles break up in flight over Hafr al-Basin. Debris showers on the town, damaging buildings and injuring residents.

FEBRUARY 14 Kuwait
The burning oil wells have created a vast black cloud that is blinding Coalition pilots.

FEBRUARY 14 Jordan
Jordan issues a statement condemning the bunker bombing in Baghdad. It announces three days of mourning for the victims. Hundreds of people march on the U.S. Embassy in Amman, the capital, in protest.

FEBRUARY 15 Iraq
Iraq says it will comply with UN Resolution 660 regarding withdrawing from Kuwait—but only

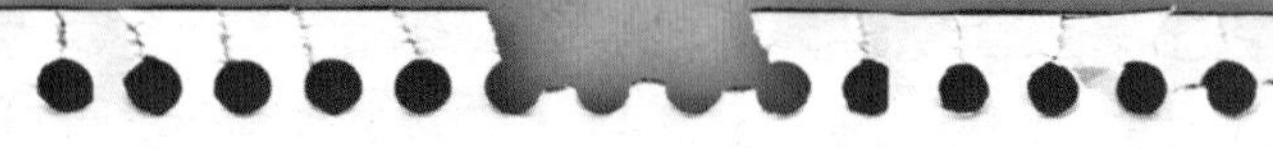

EYEWITNESS: Glenn Dixon, British Army, February 1991

"That which followed will echo in my mind forever, as 24 guns let rip at once, a barrage of Royal Artillery pumping explosive rounds toward the soon-to-be-dead, disorientated, demoralized, and neutralized enemy. It seemed to last forever. In the background was screaming, muffled explosions, and the crackling of small-arms fire and then silence again."

Small arms – weapons carried by a soldier in battle.

An Iraqi tank is blown to pieces after being hit by an antitank missile.

on condition that Israel withdraws from all occupied Palestinian territories. In addition, the Iraqis want Coalition members to pay for the rebuilding of Iraq.

FEBRUARY 15 United States
President Bush dismisses the Iraqi peace offer as a "cruel hoax." The president states: "They must withdraw without condition, there must be full implementation of all the Security Council resolutions." Bush says that the Coalition will continue its campaign "until a massive withdrawal begins."

FEBRUARY 16 Iraq
U.S. attack helicopters make their first nighttime raids on Iraqi positions. The Iraqis shoot down three U.S. aircraft. Iraqi authorities claim that 130 civilians have been killed by British bomb attacks.

FEBRUARY 16 Israel
Two Iraqi Scud missiles land in unpopulated areas. A total of 35 Scuds have now been fired at Israel since the war began.

FEBRUARY 16 United States
Iraq's ambassador to the United Nations says that his country will use weapons of mass destruction if the bombing campaign continues.

KEY PEOPLE: Norman Schwarzkopf

General Norman Schwarzkopf was the leader of Coalition forces in the Gulf. He commanded troops from over 30 countries. His plan was to fool the Iraqis into thinking he would attack Kuwait from the sea. This made the Iraqis send troops and tanks into eastern Kuwait. But when the attack came it was made in the west. So successful was Schwarzkopf's plan that the ground fighting was over in 100 hours. He retired from the U.S. Army in 1992.

Palestine – an Arab region, much of which is now controlled by Israel.

During the war, the Iraqis released dozens of mines into the Persian Gulf.

FEBRUARY 17 Saudi Arabia
U.S. and Iraqi troops clash in seven incidents along the Saudi-Kuwait border. In one incident, U.S. AH-64 Apache attack helicopters capture 20 Iraqi prisoners when they threaten to open fire on them.

FEBRUARY 18 Persian Gulf
Floating Iraqi mines strike two U.S. warships. The USS *Tripoli* and USS *Princeton* are both damaged but remain operational. Allied minesweeping operations are extended into the northern Persian Gulf.

FEBRUARY 18 Saudia Arabia
General Norman Schwarzkopf promises that the Allies will not attack the Iraqi Army if it begins withdrawing from Kuwait.

FEBRUARY 19 Kuwait
U.S. Marines bombard Iraqi targets inside Kuwait with heavy artillery fire. Coalition helicopters and land forces take more than 500 Iraqi prisoners in three ground attacks.

FEBRUARY 19 Persian Gulf
Minesweepers have found 22 mines in the northern Gulf during their operations to clear the sea routes.

FEBRUARY 19 Iraq
Coalition aircraft resume the bombing of Baghdad, the first large-scale attacks since the bunker bombing on February 13.

KEY WEAPONS: Abrams tank

The American M1 Abrams main battle tank is armed with a powerful 120-mm main gun. It is also equipped with three machine guns. The Abrams has advanced armor made of steel and ceramic, and plastics, making it difficult to destroy. Despite its 63-ton (64-tonne) weight, the Abrams has a top speed of 45 miles per hour (72 kmh). Over the course of the Gulf War, the Abrams successfully knocked out dozens of enemy tanks—but not one Abrams was destroyed by an Iraqi tank.

Minesweeper – a naval vessel that clears mines from the sea.

EYEWITNESS: General Norman Schwarzkopf, Coalition commander

"The President, the Congress, the American people, and indeed the world, stand united in their support of your actions. You are a member of the most powerful force our country in coalition with our allies has ever assembled in a single theater to face such an aggressor. You have trained hard for this battle and you are ready. I have seen in your eyes a determination to get this job done. My confidence in you is total."

FEBRUARY 19 Iran
The Iranian foreign minister says he has held discussions with his Iraqi counterparts. They have told him that Iraq has unconditionally agreed to withdraw from Kuwait. He calls for the United Nations to respond with a 48-hour ceasefire and a timetable for troop withdrawal.

FEBRUARY 20 Saudi Arabia
One American is killed and seven wounded in fighting along the Saudi border.

FEBRUARY 20 Kuwait
U.S. warplanes attack 300 Iraqi vehicles 60 miles (96 km) inside Kuwait. They destroy 28 tanks.

Two U.S. Apache attack helicopters armed with antitank missiles.

Ceasefire – a halt in the fighting.

EYEWITNESS: Jeremy Thompson, British journalist, February 1991

"We are entering the bad lands now, the soldier told his men, as they drove through the archway into a deserted town. Khafji had been known as a safe hideout for Iraqi terrorists. But now, it appeared no more than a ghost town. Every shop was shut, not a soul was on the street. In the eerie silence, evidence of a panic-stricken evacuation. The Iraqi artillery has stopped raining down on the deserted town of Khafji."

FEBRUARY 21 USSR

Soviet spokesman Vitaly Ignatenko announces that Iraq and the Soviet Union have agreed a plan that could lead to Iraq's withdrawal from Kuwait. The plan calls for the withdrawal to begin after the end of hostilities. It also calls for Iraq to be allowed to resume international trade once two-thirds of its forces have left Kuwait. In addition, all other United Nations resolutions are to be lifted once all the troops have gone. This would mean that Iraq would not have to pay compensation to Kuwait. Also, the Soviet plan does not mention restoring Kuwait's rulers to power, as called for by the United Nations.

FEBRUARY 21 Iraq

In a radio broadcast, Saddam Hussein condemns those Arab governments opposed to Iraq as traitors to their people. In his 35-minute speech, he gives no indication whether or not Iraq will accept the Soviet peace plan.

FEBRUARY 21 Persian Gulf

The USS *Wisconsin* shells and destroys an Iraqi bunker at Khafji.

FEBRUARY 22 Iraq

Iraq wants six weeks to withdraw from Kuwait.

FEBRUARY 22 Kuwait

Around 100 oil wells have been destroyed by the Iraqis in Kuwait, plus oil tanks, oil terminals, and other oil installations.

FEBRUARY 22 United States

President Bush, after consulting other members of the Coalition, rejects the Soviet–Iraqi peace plan. He tells the Iraqis they have until 17:00

A warship in the Persian Gulf bombards Iraqi positions in Kuwait.

Bunker – a fortified military position with thick walls and roof.

hours on February 23 to begin their withdrawal from Kuwait. They must complete it within one week to avoid a ground war.

Kuwaiti oil wells on fire after being blown up by Iraqi troops.

FEBRUARY 23 USSR

The Russians claim that Saddam Hussein has agreed to withdraw Iraqi troops from Kuwait immediately without conditions.

FEBRARY 23 Kuwait

There is no sign that the Iraqis are pulling out of Kuwait. But there are growing reports of atrocities committed against Kuwaitis by Iraqi soldiers. The number of sorties by Coalition warplanes over Kuwait has increased dramatically in the last 24 hours. Some 1,200 air combat missions are flown today alone. But this does not prevent the Iraqis from continuing to blow up Kuwaiti oil facilities and shipping terminals.

FEBRUARY 23 United States

The Kuwaiti ambassador to the United Nations tells the Security Council that at least 28,000 Kuwaitis have been reported as missing. It seems many of them have been taken by force to Iraq. The Department of Defense fears they may be being tortured.

KEY UNITS: Iraq's Republican Guard

The Republican Guard was originally set up to protect Saddam Hussein. It also provided the elite troops of the Iraqi Army. The Guard was organized into six divisions and various specialist combat units, and had hundreds of tanks and other armored vehicles. The troops of the Republican Guard (at right) were the best in the Iraqi Army. The destruction of Republican Guard units was a high priority of Coalition planners. In February 1991, Coalition troops fought their toughest battles against the Guard.

Atrocity – a brutal act of unprovoked violence against a civilian.

FEBRUARY 24 Kuwait and Iraq

The Allied ground campaign to free Kuwait begins at 04:00 hours. UN forces carry out a "left hook" maneuver in which their main strength is concentrated on the left flank. The Coalition attack is led by U.S. Marines, and includes troops from Britain, Saudi Arabia, Kuwait, Egypt, and Syria. Their aim is to cut off the Iraqi Army in Kuwait so it can be destroyed. Having been bombed by Allied aircraft for nearly a month, thousands of Iraqi soldiers give up rather than fight.

UN attack and transport helicopters on the first day of the ground war.

FEBRUARY 24 United States

President Bush tells Americans: "The liberation of Kuwait has entered the final phase."

FEBRUARY 24 Saudi Arabia

General Norman Schwarzkopf hails the first day of the UN ground offensive as a "dramatic success." Allied casualties are very light, but more than 5,500 Iraqis have been captured in the first 10 hours of the ground offensive. More than 300 Allied attack and supply helicopters have flown 50 miles (80 km) into Iraqi territory. It is the largest helicopter assault in military history.

KEY WEAPONS: Cruise missile

The Tomahawk cruise missile (at right) was used for the first time in the Gulf War. Some 300 missiles were launched from U.S. ships and submarines. Flying at a speed of 55 miles per hour (88 kmh), the missile uses sensors and gyroscopes to avoid obstacles and reach its target. In the Gulf War Cruise missiles attacked Iraqi antiaircraft weapons, command-and-control centers, and electrical power facilities. Around six Cruise missiles were shot down before they reached their target.

Flank – the right or left side of an army.

EYEWITNESS: Sergeant Haughton, 4th Armoured Division

"So with the battleship USS *New Jersey* moored offshore, waiting hours earlier to fire shells the size of a mini car on to the enemy coastal battery, which I now found myself standing next to, made for a sobering thought. The center of Kuwait city was a devastated, burnt shell, littered with the remains of a brutal occupation. Iraq was a bully who tried to box above his weight, only to receive a bloody nose from a highly trained opponent."

FEBRUARY 24 Israel

Two Iraqi Scud missiles land in Israel but there are no casualties.

FEBRUARY 25 Kuwait

Coalition forces reach the outskirts of Kuwait City. They are poised to liberate the capital as more reports emerge of Iraqi troops killing civilians and setting fire to buildings in the city. Four U.S. soldiers have been killed and 21 more wounded in the first two days of the UN ground assault. Nearly 20,000 Iraqis have been taken prisoner so far. In addition, Coalition forces have destroyed 270 Iraqi tanks.

A Coalition armored personnel carrier smashes through Iraqi defenses.

Armored personnel carrier – armored vehicle that carries soldiers inside.

IN FOCUS: B-52 bomber

Known as the Big Ugly Fat Fella (BUFF), the U.S. B-52 bomber (at right) can carry up to 60,000 lb (27,727 kg) of bombs. For defense against enemy fighters it has a remote-control tail turret armed with either four machine guns or a 20-mm cannon. The B-52 is powered by eight jet engines. It has a top speed of 600 miles per hour (960 kmh). In the Gulf War, B-52s were used to bomb Iraqi troops and defenses. They dropped high-explosive, antipersonnel, and antiarmor bombs.

FEBRUARY 25 Iraq

The U.S. 101st Airborne Division, which uses helicopters to move rapidly into attack, cuts Highway 8 in the Euphrates Valley, the main road from Kuwait into Iraq. The French commander in the Gulf says his troops have destroyed an entire Iraqi division, and have advanced 100 miles (160 km) into Iraq. Saddam Hussein orders his troops to make a fighting withdrawal from Kuwait.

FEBRUARY 25 Persian Gulf

An Iraqi Silkworm antiship missile is fired at USS *Missouri*. It is destroyed by missiles fired from the British ship HMS *Gloucester*.

FEBRUARY 25 Saudi Arabia

An Iraqi Scud missile is fired at Dhahran. It breaks up in the air, scattering debris over a U.S. housing compound in suburban Al Khobar. Falling debris kills 27 U.S. Army Reserve personnel and wounds 100 more.

FEBRUARY 26 Kuwait

Coalition forces have now captured 63,000 Iraqi prisoners. Resistance fighters rise up against the

Iraqi soldiers give themselves up to Coalition forces in Kuwait.

Convoy – vehicles grouped together for protection.

Iraqis in Kuwait City. U.S. Marines reach Kuwait City and liberate the U.S. Embassy. Iraqi troops begin a mass retreat from Kuwait City in any vehicles they can find. Many of the vehicles are filled with loot that includes anything the fleeing soldiers could seize in their last hours in Kuwait. However, UN aircraft halt the retreating Iraqis on the highway toward Basra. Coalition bombing bogs down the Iraqi convoy in a 4-mile (6 km) line of stationary traffic on Mutla Ridge. A reported 10,000 Iraqis die. The road to Basra becomes known as the "Highway of Death."

EYEWITNESS: Captain M. Johnson, French Army

"The first day our fire was on fixed positions and infantry which were dug into trenches and foxholes. The next day one of our units fought one Iraqi tank company of T-55 medium tanks and destroyed eight tanks out of fifteen which were there in fifteen minutes. Of the other Iraqi tanks, some were destroyed by aircraft and others by helicopters."

FEBRUARY 26 Saudi Arabia

The Kuwaiti government-in-exile says it will not accept any action from Iraq that amounts to less than a complete and unconditional Iraqi withdrawal from Kuwait.

FEBRUARY 26 Iraq

In a speech on Baghdad Radio, Saddam Hussein declares that Kuwait will always be part of Iraq, but that "current circumstances are such that armed forces are forcing us to withdraw."

FEBRUARY 26 United States

The UN Security Council meets in New York at the request of the Soviet Union. Iraq's representative says its troops have already begun withdrawing from Kuwait. Iraq wants the United Nations to arrange a ceasefire so that its troops can pull out safely. The request is rejected by a majority of the Security Council. President George Bush says that the war will continue until Iraqi forces are thrown out of Kuwait. The Coalition will not attack retreating Iraqi soldiers if they have no weapons. However, armed Iraqis will be attacked and killed.

Destroyed vehicles on the "Highway of Death" outside Kuwait City.

Exile – a forced absence from one's country.

An Iraqi tank burns after being hit by an antitank missile in Kuwait.

However, large quantities of live ammunition in the city remain a cause for concern for Coalition troops. Coalition carrier- and ground-based air attacks prevent the Iraqis rebuilding bridges and stop the Republican Guard leaving Kuwait.

FEBRUARY 27 Saudi Arabia
The authorities state that U.S. casualties since the start of the ground war are 28 killed, 89 wounded, and 5 missing in action. Total Coalition losses stand at 79 killed, 213 wounded, 35 missing, and 9 taken prisoner. The Coalition have destroyed 3,008 Iraqi tanks, 1,856 armored vehicles, and 2,140 artillery pieces.

FEBRUARY 27 Kuwait
Coalition forces enter Kuwait City and raise the Kuwaiti flag. A series of small battles continue to break out in the city, however. Coalition troops fight isolated Iraqi snipers and members of the Republican Guard. It takes two days of stiff fighting to liberate the city's airport.

FEBRUARY 27 Iraq
Some 166 Abrams tanks of the U.S. 1st Armored Division, commanded by Major General Ron

KEY PEOPLE: The Kurds

In the 1980s, Saddam Hussein launched a campaign of aggression against the Kurdish people living in northern Iraq. In March 1988, he ordered a poison gas attack in Halabja. Between 3,000 and 5,000 Kurds were killed. The Kurds rose up in revolt in February 1991 but were defeated by the Iraqis. As a result, 1.5 million Kurds fled to Turkey. The United Nations created a "safe haven" for them in northern Iraq. This zone was created to prevent further Iraqi attacks against the Kurds (at right).

Sniper – a marksman armed with a rifle.

EYEWITNESS: Major C. Clark, U.S. Army, February 1991

"From looking at it, you can tell that it's just as flat as the eye can see. So basically, we had to do some planning for combat engineers to come out here with earth-moving equipment to give us some protection from ground fire. We planned to have bulldozers, and then to investigate how hard it would be to dig into the ground to prepare bunkers for cover."

Griffiths, fight the Battle of Medina Ridge against the Iraqi Republican Guard. Although the Iraqis have tanks sheltered behind the sand ridge, the Americans suffer only one death. The Abrams destroy 186 Iraqi tanks (mostly Soviet-built T-72 and T-55 models) and 127 other armored vehicles. Only four Abrams tanks are hit and damaged. Not a single Coalition tank is destroyed in the battle.

FEBRUARY 27 Persian Gulf

Two Iraqi patrol boats are destroyed by U.S. Navy aircraft near Faylaka Island.

FEBRUARY 27 United States

U.S. President George Bush declares Kuwait liberated. He suspends all Coalition offensive operations, exactly 100 hours after the ground battle started.

Happy civilians celebrate in Kuwait City as the Iraqis flee north.

Liberate – to free from a foreign occupier.

FEBRUARY 27 United States
The UN Security Council meets to discuss Iraq's announcement that it is prepared to accept the Council's resolution on the Gulf War. At the end of a closed session the Security Council calls on Iraq to make a clear promise to abide by all Security Council resolutions relating to Kuwait. It also demands that Iraq release all prisoners of war and Kuwaiti civilians in Iraqi prisons.

Concrete Iraqi aircraft shelters destroyed by Coalition bombs.

FEBRUARY 27 Kuwait and Iraq
Coalition warplanes have flown more than 110,000 sorties in the Gulf War.

FEBRUARY 27 Saudi Arabia
General Norman Schwarzkopf says that the gates are now closed on Iraqi forces in the war zone. They have no way out. He also says that nothing stood between Coalition ground forces and Baghdad itself. He asserts that UN forces could have gone on to conquer Iraq, had they wished to do so.

FEBRUARY 28 Kuwait and Iraq
A ceasefire comes into effect at midnight. George Bush announces an end to hostilities but warns that the ceasefire depends on the Iraqis agreeing not to attack Coalition forces or fire more Scud missiles against Israel or

IN FOCUS: Casualties of War

Because Coalition forces had better weapons and equipment than the Iraqis, and control of the air, their casualties were low. The United States had more than 500,000 troops in the Gulf; their allies' forces totaled 160,000. U.S. casualties were 148 battle deaths and 145 nonbattle deaths. The British suffered 24 combat deaths, France 2, and Arab allies 39 casualties. Among Iraqi soldiers, some 100,000 died, 300,000 were wounded, 150,000 deserted, and 60,000 were captured.

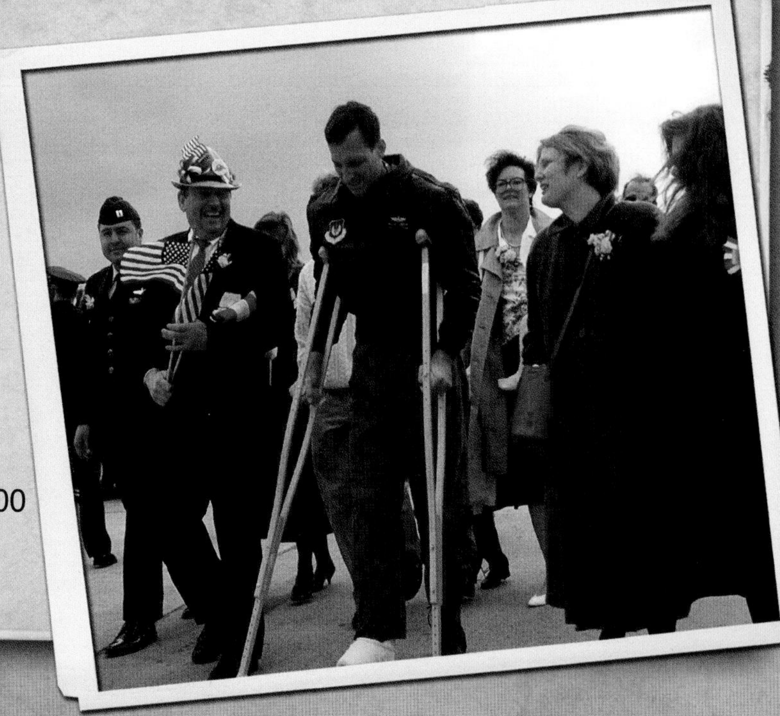

Hostilities – war or acts of aggression between two or more countries.

U.S. Marines ride north toward the Iraqi border in February 1991.

Coalition troops. They must also free all prisoners of war. If they do not, the war will continue.

FEBRUARY 28 Iraq

In a radio broadcast, Saddam Hussein tries to disguise his defeat from the Iraqi people. He declares: "The allies of Satan and its accursed leader have been taught a lesson." Most Iraqis are relieved that the war is over and that there will be no more Coalition bombing raids. The Iraqi ambassador to the United Nations meanwhile says his country will accept all UN resolutions regarding Kuwait.

EYEWITNESS: Major Jeff Tice, captured American pilot in Iraq

"This gray-haired gentleman opens up my cell door and says, 'Do you need anything?' I said, 'Yes, I could use a couple of blankets. I would like some shoes.' I hadn't had any shoes. I was wearing yellow pajamas now that didn't fit. I figured, I'd better ask now. I may not get anything ever again. So I started asking for stuff and he says, 'Don't worry. You won't need any of that. You'll be going home in 15 minutes.'"

Prisoner of war – a soldier captured during battle.

KEY PEOPLE: The Marsh Arabs

After Coalition forces drove Iraqi troops from Kuwait in the Gulf War, the Marsh Arabs in the south of Iraq rebelled. They wanted to be free from Iraqi rule. However, Iraqi government forces put down the uprisings brutally, bombing civilians from military helicopters. Between 30,000 and 60,000 Marsh Arabs died. In August 1992, U.S., British, and French forces set up a "no-fly zone" to stop attacks on Marsh Arabs (at right) from the air. However, Iraqi soldiers still attacked them on the ground.

MARCH 2 United States

The UN Security Council sets out ceasefire terms. These require Iraq to end all fighting, to leave Kuwait, to reveal information about chemical and biological weapons, to release all prisoners, and to accept responsibility for all losses resulting from its occupation of Kuwait.

MARCH 3 Iraq

General Norman Schwarzkopf dictates terms to end the six-week war. Having lost more than 60,000 of their soldiers as prisoners, and thousands more dead, the Iraqis agree. Iraq has to accept the setting up of "no-fly zones" over its territory, where only UN aircraft can operate. UN teams will visit Iraq to inspect its weapons programs. The limits imposed on Iraqi trade by the United Nations will continue.

UN food supplies are taken from a helicopter to give to the Kurds.

MARCH 17 United States

The U.S. Department of Defense announces that the first troops to return from the Gulf will be from the 24th Infantry Division.

APRIL 5 United States

President Bush announces that U.S. aircraft will drop supplies to Kurdish refugees in Turkey and northern Iraq, who are under attack by the Iraqis.

APRIL 6 Turkey

Iraq accepts the United Nations terms for a ceasefire. The First Gulf War is over.

Demilitarized zone – an area kept free of weapons and soldiers.

EYEWITNESS: U.S. General Colin Powell on the Kurdish and Marsh Arab uprisings

"The only issue that came up was should we do something about the Iraqi helicopters? It had never been one of our objectives to get involved in this kind of civil uprising between factions within Iraq and the Iraqi government. And so it was not clear what purpose would have been achieved by getting ourselves mixed up in that."

APRIL 6 Turkey

Task Force Provide Comfort is formed. U.S. cargo and fighter aircraft are flown to bases in southern Turkey. They begin delivering humanitarian aid supplies to the Kurds. Over a period of a few weeks a U.S.-led international force will be sent into northern Iraq. Resettlement areas will be constructed and a demilitarized zone established for the protection of the Kurds from the Iraqis.

APRIL 7 Iraq

U.S. transport aircraft deliver 72,000 pounds (32,727 kilograms) of supplies during Operation Provide Comfort missions to the Kurds.

APRIL 20 Iraq

The construction of the first Provide Comfort tent city begins near Zakhu, northern Iraq.

General Schwarzkopf (far left) dictates ceasefire terms to the Iraqis.

Humanitarian aid – food and medicine supplied to civilians.

Glossary

armored personnel carrier: armored vehicle that carries soldiers inside

atrocity: a brutal act of unprovoked violence against a civilian

B-52: U.S. eight-engined heavy bomber

battleship: a large, heavily armed warship

blockade: to stop enemy ships leaving their ports

bunker: a fortified military position with thick walls and roof

ceasefire: a halt in the fighting

CIA: Central Intelligence Agency, a U.S. spy organization

coalition: an alliance of nations

compound: a walled-in area

conscript: a civilian drafted into the army

convoy: vehicles grouped together for protection

demilitarized zone: an area kept free of weapons and soldiers

dictator: a ruler who has no restraints on his or her power

division: a military unit of 15,000 to 20,000 soldiers

dogfight: combat between fighter aircraft

exile: a forced absence from one's country

flak jacket: a jacket that includes bullet-proof armor

flank: the right or left side of an army

FROG missile: a short-range battlefield missile

guidance system: computers and sensors that steer a missile

hostage: a person held captive against his or her will

hostilities: war or acts of aggression between two or more countries

humanitarian aid: food and medicine supplied to civilians

Joint Chiefs: a group of officers from each branch of the U.S. armed forces

killing zone: an area of the battlefield always covered by enemy fire

landmine: a container filled with explosives that is buried in the ground

liberate: to free from a foreign occupier

mechanized: describing military forces that are transported in vehicles

minesweeper: a naval vessel that clears mines from the sea

nonaggression: a refusal to use force

Palestine: an Arab region, much of which is now controlled by Israel

prisoner of war: a soldier captured during battle

refugee: a civilian who flees a war zone

reservist: part-time soldier

small arms: weapons carried by a soldier in battle

sniper: a marksman armed with a rifle

sortie: a mission flown by a warplane

special forces: soldiers trained to fight behind enemy lines

terrorist: an extremist who uses violence against civilians

Further resources

BOOKS ABOUT THE FIRST GULF WAR

The Persian Gulf War: "The Mother of All Battles" (American War Series) by Zachary Kent, Enslow Publishers, 2000.

The Gulf War (Library Binding) by John King, Dillon Press, 1991.

Desert Storm: The First Persian Gulf War in American History (In American History) by Debra McArthur, Enslow Publishers, 2004.

American War Library—The Persian Gulf War: The War Against Iraq (American War Library) by Don Nardo, Lucent Books, 2000.

People at the Center of—The Persian Gulf War (People at the Center of) by Donna Schaffer and Alfred Meyer, Blackbirch Press, 2003.

American War Library—Weapons of War: The Persian Gulf (American War Library) by Jay R. Speakman, Lucent Books, 2000.

USEFUL WEBSITES

www.pbs.org/wgbh/pages/frontline/gulf

www.cnn.com/SPECIALS/2001/gulf.war

www.usatoday.com/news/index/iraq

www.britains-smallwars.com/gulf

www.indepthinfo.com/iraq

www.jewishvirtuallibrary.org/jsource/History/Gulf_War

Index